Year of the Reader!

Creative Activities
To Promote Reading Excitement

Written and Illustrated
by
Jan Grubb Philpot

Incentive Publications, Inc.
Nashville, Tennessee

Cover by Jan Grubb Philpot
Edited by Jan Keeling

ISBN 0-86530-247-2

Table of Contents

Preface

It's no secret that the spotlight in education these days is focused on literature and the whole language approach. *Year of the Reader!* was written to provide an organizational thread to run throughout your school year. It will add spice to your program, and is filled with unique ideas to keep the focus on literature fresh and exciting. It is a collection of thematic plans, displays, bibliographies, activities, and programs for every month. Care has been taken to provide you with ideas that meet the qualifications of any good literature-based program—literature extensions, alternative book reporting, read-aloud programs, silent sustained reading, critical reading habits, parent involvement, etc. Best of all, the book is complete with step-by-step directions, announcements, awards, parent correspondence, and other aids that make each idea a snap to use! Put the focus on literature in YOUR classroom by signing your students up for YEAR OF THE READER!

Happy Reading!

DOES THE SHOE FIT?

Getting in STEP!

Teachers around the country are recognizing the need to incorporate literature into the curriculum in order to foster a generation of readers and writers. Make this year the year you focus on developing a love of reading among your students! Start by examining "Does the Shoe Fit?" on the previous page. Use the Teacher's Literature Planner on page 13 to write down those areas you would like to strengthen. Then use the following ideas as launching pads for your own creative techniques!

1 **To make reading "special," set up a designated "reading corner" in your classroom.** You are limited only by the limits of your own creativity, and by the amount of available space.

The reading corner may be theme-oriented. For example, design a "Reading Corral" that includes a trading post (where books can be exchanged) and a telegram office (where short "telegram-like" book-sharing forms can be filled out).

You might include in your reading corner a listening station (for pre-recorded stories), or a writing center with lots of "neat" supplies and story

starters. Or link books with art, and include lots of supplies for designing book jackets or book illustrations.

Create displays in your reading corner! Grocery stores are great sources of "neat" display racks and cardboard display models. Ask the store manager if you might have some racks when they are no longer needed at the store.

Spice up your reading corner with wall murals. If your principal doesn't mind, you might have these painted on the walls. Your own students may be capable of painting murals, or contact a local high school art department. Many high school students would love to volunteer their time and talent for the "thrill" of having their work permanently displayed in a school building—or perhaps to receive extra credit from their teacher.

But reading corners need not be elaborate, only comfortable and inviting. Ask a carpet retailer to donate a carpet remnant, pile in a few pillows or stuffed animals, and you're in business!

2 Having books in the classroom is every bit as important as having them in your home, whether you have a well-stocked school media center or not. These books DO NOT take the place of the well-stocked media center—they SUPPLEMENT IT! The benefit of having books in the classroom is that the books are always where they might be idly picked up, always accessible to any potential reader. Here are some ways to obtain books for your classroom:

• Ask your librarian to pass book discards your way. The fact that a book is no longer needed in a media center does not mean it cannot be valuable in a classroom. If the binding is irreparable, remove the pages, punch holes in them, and put them in a three-ring binder. Books that have been marked with ink or markers might still have illustrations that can be cut out for flannelboard stories or used for story-starters in creative writing classes.

• Yard sales and garage sales are great places to pick up children's books at exceptionally reasonable prices. Ask your students' parents to be watching for bargains!

• Participate in a book club. This will encourage your students to build personal collections, and YOU will receive bonus books free of charge!

• Librarians frequently receive a good number of free books as enticements to host book fairs. Because these books are usually paperbacks, your librarian might be willing to part with a few—all she or he can say is "no"! (Or "yes"!)

• Encourage students to make gifts of their old books (with parental permission, of course) to the classroom. Place a bookplate in the front of each book crediting the student with the donation. Students might also have old issues of children's magazines to donate.

• If you don't mind day-old newspapers (and there are many activities using newspapers that don't require currency), ask a parent to send you a day-old copy each day. Also check to see if there is a "Newspapers in Education" program in your town. Under this program, corporate sponsors in your community foot the bill for enough daily newspapers for an entire class!

3 **With all the emphasis on thematic units and the incorporation of books into content areas, your librarian has become indispensable.** Many school libraries are becoming computerized now, and with the touch of a button, you can have a bibliography in your hands listing all materials in the media center on a specific subject. You might also ask to borrow *Children's Catalog* (a librarian's reference tool published by H.W. Wilson Co.). This book has a subject index and annotations that make it invaluable when planning theme-oriented units. *Granger's Index to Poetry* will help you discover correlating poetry.

4 **READ ALOUD.** All students, no matter how old, love being read to. Any librarian will tell you: a teacher who reads a book aloud to her classroom is the best "book salesperson" there is! Often a read-aloud title will be "checked out" for the rest of the year! It helps to know children's book preferences. Children love humorous fiction, fast-paced and with plenty of surprises. They also love mysteries. Not all books do make good read-aloud books. A bibliography of good read-aloud books for the intermediate grades is furnished below.

Armstrong, *Sounder*. Harper and Row.

Chase, *The Grandfather Tales*. Houghton Mifflin.

Cleary, *Ramona Forever*. Morrow.

Dahl, *James and the Giant Peach*. Random House.

Fleischman, *The Whipping Boy*. Morrow.

Fox, *One-Eyed Cat*. Bradbury.

Gilson, *No Coins, Please*. Morrow.

Lewis, *The Lion, the Witch and the Wardrobe*. MacMillan.

Mathis, *The Hundred Penny Box*. Puffin.

Norton, *The Borrowers*. Harcourt, Brace, Jovanovich.

O'Brien, *Mrs. Frisby and the Rats of NIMH*. Atheneum.

O'Dell, *Island of the Blue Dolphins*. Houghton.

Peck, *Soup*. Random House.

Rawls, *Where the Red Fern Grows*. Doubleday.

Robinson, *The Best Christmas Pageant Ever*. Harper and Row.

Van Allsburg, *Jumanji*. Houghton Mifflin.

Wagner, *J.T.* Dell.

White, *Charlotte's Web*. Harper.

Zemach, *Duffy and the Devil*. Farrar, Straus, Giroux.

5 The traditional book report is often threatening or boring to a child. Encourage alternative methods of book-sharing: interviews with characters, a report given in the form of a newscast, a "newspaper article"—the possibilities are endless. An excellent source of ideas is *One For the Books* by Richards and Standley (Incentive, 1984).

6 READING GOALS. Put the spotlight on reading by participating in a planned reading program. One of the better-known sponsors of such a program is World Book Encyclopedia. This company actually provides books for the classroom in exchange for participation in the program. If you don't wish to have a corporate sponsor, or you simply want to "spice up" your program, use the theme-oriented programs in *Readers' Clubhouse* (Jan Philpot, Incentive, 1991). Whatever program you choose, you'll find that providing goals often incites even the most ambivalent reader to read!

7 LITERATURE EXTENSIONS. Literature extensions make a child's experience with a book more meaningful! Dine on pasta after reading *Strega Nona*. Make a commercial "selling" the peddler's *Caps for Sale*. Create a collage *Snowy Day* of a child's own backyard. The possibilities are endless, and limited only by your own imagination!

8 **Sustained silent reading is necessary for a reader's growth and often it never happens unless instigated in the classroom.** Make it a rule in YOUR classroom that each student keep a "pleasure" book in his or her desk always, ready to be taken out at a moment's notice when work is done or "Quiet Reading Time" is announced. Allow 10-15 minutes a day for a silent reading period that is as scheduled and predictable as recess or lunchtime. Occasionally the entire school might participate in a "Readers' Alert" in which the bell is rung—not for recess, but to alert *everyone* in the building that it is time to take out those books and READ!

9 **Occasionally show audiovisual versions of a book.** Read the book first, then show the audiovisual. Have students compare the two versions! If your school library does not have a good selection of audiovisual material, check with your public library. Often public libraries are able to obtain virtually any audiovisual material you

wish through interlibrary loan from a central location. You may be charged for postage only, and in some cases, not even that. Also, many video rental stores do not charge schools for video-tape rental.

10 **Make parents a part of your literature program!** Keep them informed of ways they can encourage reading at home. Start off your year on the right foot by letting parents know that YOUR class focuses on the development of good reading habits. Send home the "Let's Raise a Reader" parent letter (page 14) soon after school begins, and keep parents periodically informed of literature happenings in your classroom with newsletters and with the parent correspondence forms included in this book!

11 **Most of all, use the ideas in this book and others, as well as your own ideas,** to make reading your focus, month-by-month, all year long! Happy reading!

Teacher's Literature Planner for month of

_____

Authors' birthdays this month:
Author   Titles to share

Book bait plans: (audiovisual, book talks, contests, quizzes, programs, etc.)

Read - aloud plans:

Bibliographies to request:

Books for the Season	Literature Extensions / Curriculum Integration

Reading Corner / Learning Center Plans:

Bulletin board / Display Plans:	Notes:

Dear _____ ,

This year is the "Year of the Reader" in my classroom! Exciting events and activities have been planned for all year long to get (and keep!) my students focused on books and reading. Because the adults in a child's life have so much influence in this area, I'd like to ask you to be my "Partners in Raising Readers."

Here are some ways you can help:

- Keep a variety of print materials in the home, including books, newspapers, and magazines.

- Read aloud to your child 10-15 minutes a day.

- Introduce your child to the public library. Make a trip to the library a weekly family outing! Children's programs at the library are scheduled at these times:

_____

_____

- Help your child build a personal library. Books may be purchased from bookstores, book clubs, book fairs, yard sales, or your child may receive books other members of the family have outgrown.

- Encourage your child to talk about books, and about our classroom programs.

- When you rent a videotape, get one based on a children's book!

- Don't criticize your child's reading habits. He may read a comic book—this is pleasure reading! She may read a baseball card guide—this is reading for information!

- Let your children see YOU reading!

I'll keep you informed of classroom activities throughout the year. If your child doesn't already love to read—*this* may be the year we raise a reader!

Sincerely,

The READER'S BREAKFAST CLUB!

A Reader's Breakfast Club is a great way to start the day for you AND your students! Its purpose is to introduce students to the habit of reading the daily newspaper—but it has the added benefits of making students feel very special and of helping you build rapport with your students in small groups. It can be a month-long activity or an all-year-long activity!

PLANNING SUGGESTIONS:

1 **Locate enough daily newspapers for 5-6 students to share each morning.** If you have a Newspapers in Education program in your city, you are in luck! Under the NIE program, corporate sponsors foot the bill for providing daily newspapers to classrooms. Check with your librarian to see if such a program exists in your area. If not, you might ask a local newspaper publisher to donate several daily copies (or ask parents to help).

2 **Invite 5 or 6 of your students to be your guests in a morning Reader's Breakfast Club for a week.** (You might draw lots to determine who will be asked each time). Use the invitation on page 17. The students should arrive at school early, breakfast in tow.

Hint: You might also want to arrange for local businesses or fast-food restaurants to furnish breakfast for the students during this program. Businesses can be amazingly cooperative when they are intrigued with a unique educational program.

Each week meet with a fresh batch of Breakfast Club participants until each student has had a chance to participate.

3 Use your Breakfast Club time to munch breakfast together while reading and discussing the daily news. There are also a variety of educational newspaper activities that could be engaged in each day. For example:

- Have students read an article and answer the 5 W's and H the reporter has used to make an informational article (Who? What? When? Where? Why? How?)

- Make a list of questions that could be answered by perusing a particular section of the paper. Let students have a "scavenger hunt" to find answers.

- Have students find an example of each of the following: national news, state news, local news.

- Have students examine advertisements and look for the special words or phrases that are used to "sell."

- Have students put the day's headlines in alphabetical order.

- Have students find an example of news about each of the following: a political figure, an artist or writer, an entertainer, a sports figure, etc.

The list of possibilities is endless and limited only by the limits of your own imagination. NIE programs also typically offer, usually free of charge, teacher's activity guides.

4 At the conclusion of each group's participation give each Breakfast Club member an award (page 17).

5 Be sure to thank any businesses who helped to sponsor your program! It is a good idea to publicize business help or donations: by having the local newspaper include the information in an article about your program, by posting an appreciation notice prominently in the school, by making a large "thank-you" banner (signed by all participating students) to go in the front window of an office or store, or by sending notes to parents informing them of business cooperation. Businesses will appreciate the publicity and you will find them more willing to help you at other times!

Dear _____,

You are invited to join me each morning at ____ (time) from ____ (date) to ____ (date) for the **READER'S BREAKFAST CLUB!**

We will enjoy breakfast together while we read and discuss the daily news!

Your teacher,

✔ ☐ bring breakfast with you
☐ breakfast will be provided.

<u>So Glad</u> you were a part of my **READER'S BREAKFAST CLUB!**

I hope you enjoyed it as much as I did and I hope you make reading the newspaper _a daily habit!_

Teacher _____   date _____

A Bulletin Board bibliography to motivate readers!

A seasonal bulletin board for you! Use the information provided to plan thematic units, classroom correlations, and for read-aloud plans. Use the display to spark reading interest in your students.

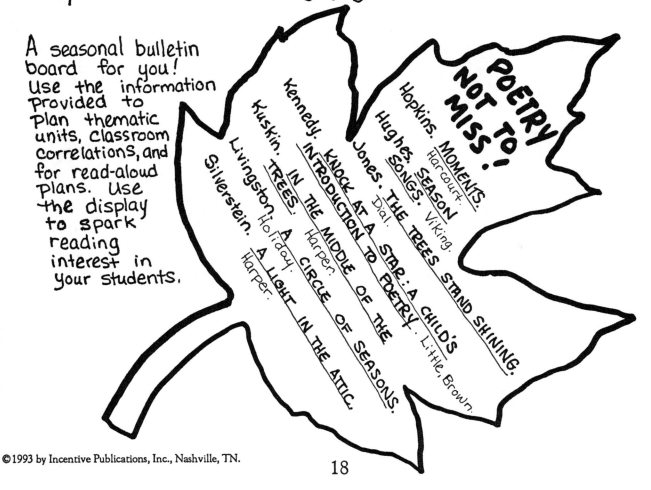

POETRY NOT TO MISS!

Hopkins. MOMENTS. Harcourt.

Hughes. SEASON SONGS. Viking.

Jones. THE TREES STAND SHINING. Dial.

Kennedy. KNOCK AT A STAR: A CHILD'S INTRODUCTION TO POETRY. Little, Brown.

Kuskin. IN THE MIDDLE OF THE TREES. Harper.

Livingston. A CIRCLE OF SEASONS. Holiday.

Silverstein. A LIGHT IN THE ATTIC. Harper.

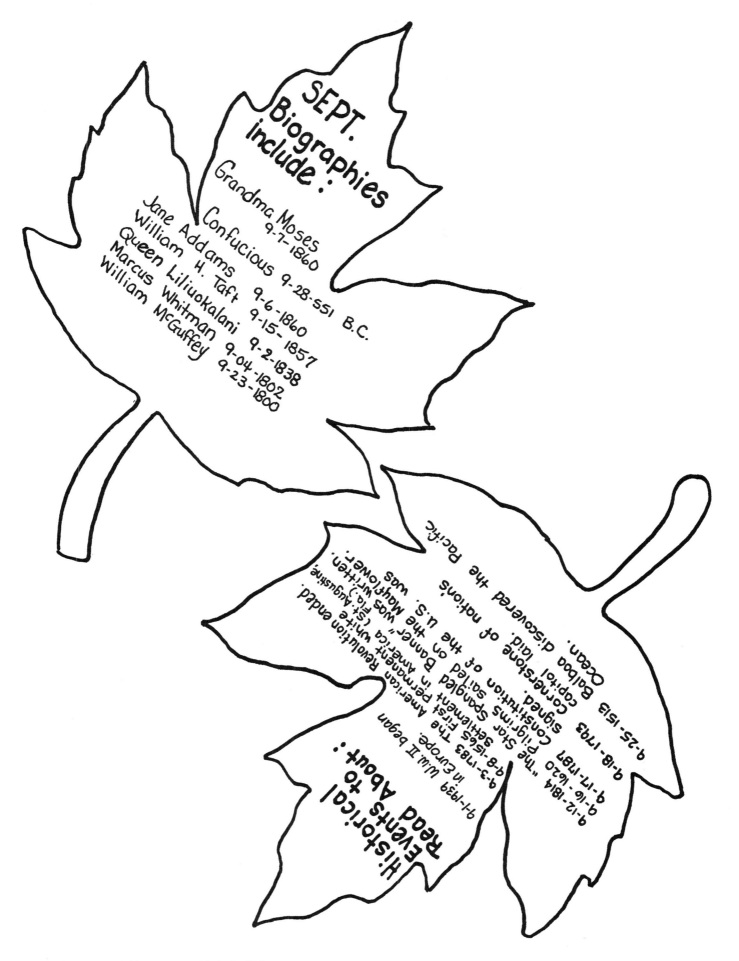

SEPT.
Biographies
include:

Grandma Moses
9-7-1860

Confucious 9-28-551 B.C.

Jane Addams 9-6-1860
William H. Taft 9-15-1857
Queen Liliuokalani 9-2-1838
Marcus Whitman 9-04-1802
William McGuffey 9-23-1800

Historical
Events to
Read About:

9-1-1939 WW II began
in Europe.

4-3-1783 "The American Revolution ended.

4-8-1565 First permanent settlement in America (St. Augustine, Fla.) was written.

9-12-1814 The Star Spangled Banner" was written.

9-16-1620 Pilgrims sailed on the Mayflower.

9-17-1787 Constitution of the U.S. was signed.

9-18-1793 Cornerstone of nations' capitol laid.

9-25-1513 Balboa discovered the Pacific Ocean.

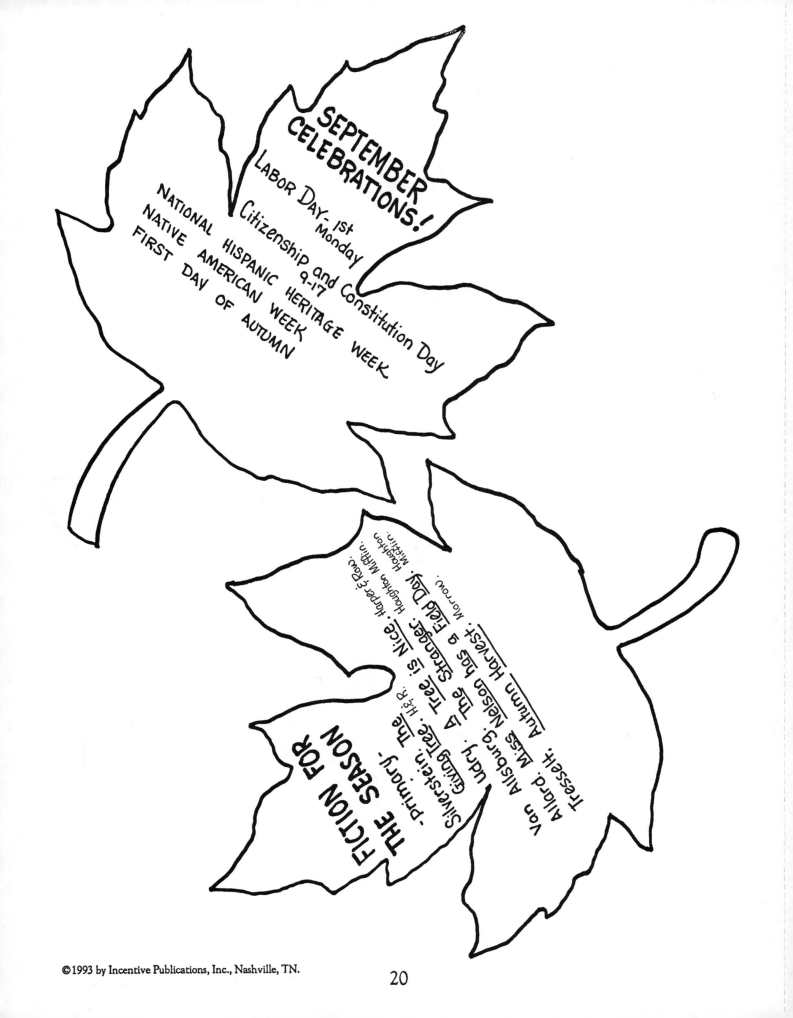

SEPTEMBER CELEBRATIONS!

Labor Day - 1st Monday

Citizenship and Constitution Day 9-17

NATIONAL HISPANIC HERITAGE WEEK

NATIVE AMERICAN WEEK

FIRST DAY OF AUTUMN

FICTION FOR THE SEASON

Van Allsburg, Chris. *The Stranger*. Houghton Mifflin.

Miss Nelson has a Field Day. Houghton Mifflin.

Udry. *A Tree is Nice*. Harper & Row.

Silverstein. *The Giving Tree*. Harper & Row.

Tresselt. *Autumn Harvest*. Morrow.

- Primary.

IN SEPTEMBER

Get acquainted with your

LIBRARY!

Students! Let's get acquainted with our library! Use the space below to draw a floor plan of the library. Be sure to label all of the following: card catalog, check-out desk, return desk, fiction, easy books, nonfiction, biography, reference, magazines, vertical file, paperbacks, audiovisual, listening carrels, audiovisual viewing area . . . and anything else special or unique to YOUR library!

Name(s)

I'M A READER TO THE CORE!

Student writes about the beginning of the book on this apple.

Make book reporting more "AP-PEELING" and brighten up your classroom with these attractive mobiles!

Run off copies of "I'm a Reader to the Core!" on bright green paper. Apples may be duplicated on red paper or white. (If white, color "skin" red.)

Student writes about the "middle" of the book or most exciting part on this apple.

Hint: This apple is easier done if run on red paper and stem and "bite" painted or chalked in green and white. "Set" chalk with hairspray.

Punch holes where indicated, string together with yarn & suspend from ceiling for a colorful autumn display!

I'M A READER TO THE CORE!

Student writes conclusion of book on this apple.

Run on white paper. Use markers, paint or chalk to make red and green parts of apples

Bulletin board idea

hints: - use real ribbons on baskets.
- cut out extra "leaves" and use on outside
of bulletin board as a border.

The Giving Tree by Shel Silverstein (Harper and Row, 1964) is an excellent book to bring into the primary curriculum during the fall season. Use the following ideas for lessons in "Gifts from the Trees."

Objectives:
1. Students will come up with a list of the contributions of trees to our lives.
2. Students will recognize pictures of items whose existence would not be possible without trees.
3. Students will participate in the creation of a class collage, "Gifts from the Trees" (see above bulletin board).

Materials: *The Giving Tree* by Shel Silverstein, blackboard, patterns of leaves, scissors, glue sticks, old magazines.

Procedure:
1. Introduce and read the book *The Giving Tree*.
2. Ask students to orally review the gifts of the tree in the book. List these on the board.

3. Have students brainstorm a list of other things that are possible only because there are trees. List these.

4. Explain to the class members that they will make a bulletin board collage called "Gifts of the Trees." Each student should be given two or three leaf patterns. Students are to locate a picture of a "gift from the trees" in an old magazine and paste it to the leaf pattern.

5. Divide the class into groups. Give each group leaf patterns, scissors, glue sticks, and a stack of old magazines (hint: your librarian may be willing to donate some of these, or parents may send some from home).

6. Have groups attach leaves to bulletin board as shown on the previous page.

7. Have each child share with the class items he or she found that are "gifts from trees"—attach them to your bulletin board display.

8. As a follow-up activity, you may announce to the class that on Arbor Day they will be returning a gift to nature by giving a young tree a safe place to grow. Make plans for an upcoming class celebration during which the class will plant a new tree on school grounds.

Suggested supplementary literature:
Udry, Janice, *A Tree is Nice.* (Harper and Row, 1956)
"Trees," a poem by Joyce Kilmer.

Hint: trees to plant may be donated by a local nursery or the U.S. Forestry Service. Be sure to type in credit for your source at the bottom of the announcement.

In honor of the gifts trees have given us

_____'s class at

_____
School

will be returning a gift to nature by planting a tree on school grounds. You are invited to attend!

date: _____
time: _____

an announcement for other classes, parents, and the press!

LEAF PATTERNS
TO REPRODUCE
FOR THE GIVING
TREE ACTIVITY.

A bulletin board bibliography to motivate readers!

A seasonal bulletin board for you! Use the information provided to plan thematic units and classroom correlations. Use the bulletin board display to spark reading interest in your students!

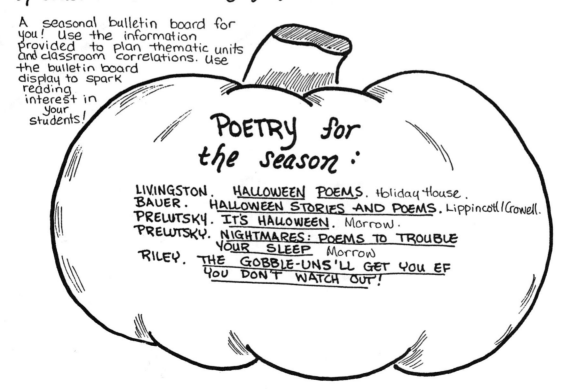

POETRY for the season:

LIVINGSTON. HALLOWEEN POEMS. Holiday House.
BAUER. HALLOWEEN STORIES AND POEMS. Lippincott/Crowell.
PRELUTSKY. IT'S HALLOWEEN. Morrow.
PRELUTSKY. NIGHTMARES: POEMS TO TROUBLE YOUR SLEEP Morrow
RILEY. THE GOBBLE-UNS'LL GET YOU EF YOU DON'T WATCH OUT!

OCTOBER CELEBRATIONS!

NATIONAL FIRE PREVENTION WEEK

CANADIAN THANKSGIVING DAY
COLUMBUS DAY · OCT. 12
OCT. 31 - HALLOWEEN

FICTION FOR THE SEASON *(primary)*

ADAMS. <u>A HALLOWEEN HAPPENING</u>. Macmillan.
BROWN. <u>ARTHUR'S HALLOWEEN</u>. Atlantic.
BALIAN. <u>HUMBUG WITCH</u>. Abington.
MILLER. <u>MOUSEKIN'S GOLDEN HOUSE</u> Prentice Hall.
STEVENSON. <u>THAT TERRIBLE HALLOWEEN NIGHT</u>.
Greenwillow.

OCTOBER BIOGRAPHIES
INCLUDE:

10-1-1924	JIMMY CARTER
10-2-1869	MOHANDAS GANDHI
10-5-1829	CHESTER A. ARTHUR
10-6-1820	JENNY LIND
10-11-1884	ELEANOR ROOSEVELT
10-14-1644	WILLIAM PENN
10-14-1890	DWIGHT D. EISENHOWER
10-16-1758	NOAH WEBSTER
10-25-1881	PABLO PICASSO
10-25-1888	RICHARD E. BYRD
10-27-1858	THEODORE ROOSEVELT
10-30-1735	JOHN ADAMS

HISTORICAL EVENTS TO READ ABOUT:

10-8-1871	GREAT CHICAGO FIRE
10-12-1492	COLUMBUS LANDED IN AMERICA
10-17-1859	JOHN BROWN'S RAID
10-19-1781	BRITISH SURRENDERED AT YORKTOWN
10-19-1879	THOMAS EDISON DEMONSTRATED THE ELECTRIC LIGHT
10-21-1520	MAGELLAN ENTERED STRAIT NAMED FOR HIM
10-24-1945	UNITED NATIONS ESTABLISHED
10-28-1886	STATUE OF LIBERTY DEDICATED
10-31-1864	NEVADA, 36TH STATE

Bulletin board idea

CATCH THE READING SPIRIT!

CATCH THE READING SPIRIT! is a good activity to involve the entire school (or a grade level) in a reading and listening activity for the month of October. It is a read-aloud book promotion with the added benefits of school involvement and the building of listening skills. Each day students will listen to a book chapter read over the school intercom. Each day should feature a different "Mystery Reader." As they listen, the students will try to determine the identity of the "Mystery Reader"!

Here's how to have a successful program:

1 Decide whether the program will involve the entire school, a grade level, or just an individual classroom. Make plans with the professionals in your school.

2 Choose a good read-aloud book that most of the children will enjoy. A humorous work of fiction or a mystery would be a good choice.

3 Line up each day's "Mystery Reader." You'll need one reader per chapter, and you'll need to choose people with whom the children are familiar: the principal, other teachers, janitors, aides, lunchroom staff, etc. In order to make the readings more convenient for all your "Mystery Readers," you may choose to have them tape-record their readings.

4 Announce your "Catch the Reading Spirit" program to the students. You may use the form on page 35. The bulletin board on page 31 would be a nice display (and good P.R. for your program) in a school hallway. A "Reading Spirit" pattern is provided on page 34. Be sure each student has a form (page 36) on which to write daily guesses of the Mystery Reader's identity. If there are not enough lines on the form, be sure to add lines so that there is one line for each chapter of the book.

5 On the designated day, play your recording of the first chapter via the school intercom so that participating classes can hear it. (Most intercom systems can be turned off in designated areas or rooms. If you have chosen not to include other classrooms, you may simply play the recording in your own room.)

6 At the end of your program, unveil the list of "Mystery Readers." Give each student who correctly identified all (or most) of your Mystery Readers an award (and perhaps a "mystery prize"—a paperback mystery book!). Don't forget to send the "Mystery Readers" a thank-you (page 33). WARNING: The book chosen for this activity will probably remain checked out from the library for the rest of the year!

THANK YOU for being a MYSTERY READER in our "CATCH THE READING SPIRIT" Program!

A THANK-YOU FOR READERS!

THANK YOU for being a **MYSTERY READER** in our "CATCH THE READING SPIRIT" Program!

date_____

signature_____

You did a **BOO-TIFUL** job **CATCHING THE READING SPIRIT** by guessing the identities of our MYSTERY READERS! Congratulations!

signature_____

date_____

A reward for Listeners!

A "READING SPIRIT" for the bulletin board on p. 31.

Hint: at the end of the program, put the readers' photos in place of the books in the ghosts' hands, or simply write their names on the books.

Attach real rope or yarn here.
↓

CATCH THE READING SPIRIT!

HEY KIDS!

This month you are invited to CATCH THE READING SPIRIT by listening to the book _____ by _____. It will be read by a different MYSTERY READER each day. MYSTERY READERS may be anyone on our school's staff. Keep track of your guess of the day's MYSTERY READER on the form given you by your teacher. A "MYSTERY" prize for each student guessing all (or the most) mystery identities correctly.

HAPPY LISTENING!

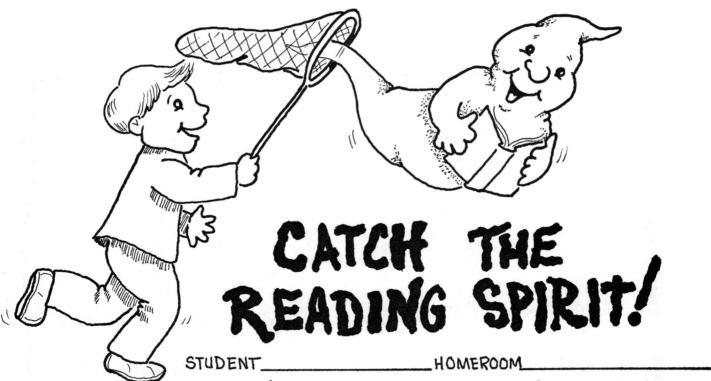

CATCH THE READING SPIRIT!

STUDENT_____ HOMEROOM_____

Students! Fill in your guess of the day's
mystery READER below!

DATE	MYSTERY READER
1. _____	_____
2. _____	_____
3. _____	_____
4. _____	_____
5. _____	_____
6. _____	_____
7. _____	_____
8. _____	_____
9. _____	_____
10. _____	_____

A bulletin board bibliography to motivate readers!

Get the HANG of good reading in November!

FICTION FOR THE SEASON

NOV. BIOGRAPHIES

POETRY

HISTORICAL EVENTS TO READ ABOUT

NOV. CELEBRATIONS

A seasonal bulletin board for you! Use the information provided to plan thematic units and classroom correlations. Use the bulletin board display to spark reading interest in your students!

Poetry for the Season:

Hopkins. MERRILY COMES OUR HARVEST IN. Harcourt, B.,J.

Livingston. THANKSGIVING POEMS. Holiday House.

Prelutsky. It's THANKSGIVING. Greenwillow.

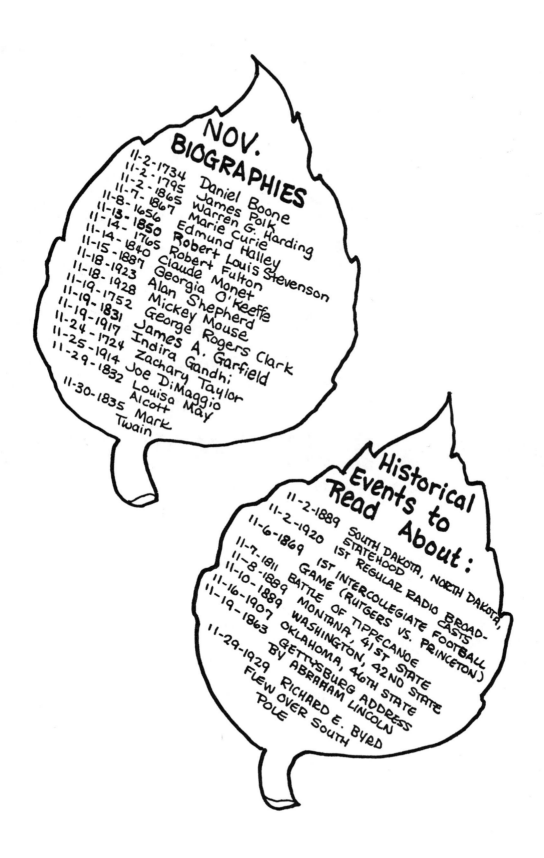

NOV. BIOGRAPHIES

Date	Name
11-2-1734	Daniel Boone
11-2-1795	James Polk
11-2-1865	Warren G. Harding
11-7-1867	Marie Curie
11-8-1656	Edmund Halley
11-13-1850	Robert Louis Stevenson
11-14-1765	Robert Fulton
11-14-1840	Claude Monet
11-15-1887	Georgia O'Keeffe
11-18-1923	Alan Shepherd
11-18-1928	Mickey Mouse
11-19-1752	George Rogers Clark
11-19-1831	James A. Garfield
11-19-1917	Indira Gandhi
11-24-1724	Zachary Taylor
11-25-1914	Joe DiMaggio
11-29-1832	Louisa May Alcott
11-30-1835	Mark Twain

Historical Events to Read About:

11-2-1889	South Dakota, North Dakota, Statehood
11-2-1920	1st Regular Radio Broadcasts
11-6-1869	1st Intercollegiate Football Game (Rutgers vs. Princeton)
11-7-1811	Battle of Tippecanoe
11-8-1889	Montana, 41st State
11-10-1889	Washington, 42nd State
11-16-1907	Oklahoma, 46th State
11-19-1863	Gettysburg Address by Abraham Lincoln
11-29-1929	Richard E. Byrd Flew Over South Pole

November Book-a-tivity
A VOTE FOR THE BOOKS!

Have students campaign for books by holding a mock election in November! Here's how:

1 This is a good month to present a lesson on the meaning of democracy and voting privileges and responsibilities. Explain terms such as parties, caucus, campaign, platform, nomination, primary, ballot.

2 Divide your class into "parties." Let the parties "caucus" and come up with a book nomination for a School or Grade Favorite. Explain that in order to present a good "platform," they will have to be very familiar with the book. Suggest the students reread the book and work together on the "Platform Worksheet" (page 42).

3 It's campaign time! Parties can vie for votes in a number of ways:
• Campaign speeches (booktalks) given in various classrooms.
• Videotaped campaign ads "selling" voters on their book. This is especially fun if you have a closed circuit TV system in your school.
• Campaign posters hung in the halls of the school.
• Campaign cards. Students can talk to others about the book during breaks or at recess time, and pass out cards.

Remind students this is a "clean" election—no mud-slinging allowed!

4 It's election time! Make up a voting booth, using a refrigerator box and a ballot box. Have a precinct worker hand each voter one ballot as he or she enters the booth. Decorate your voting corner with red, white, and blue streamers! (Hint: it may be possible to borrow a *real* voting machine!)

5 Only teachers may count the returns! Announce the winner over the school intercom. Read the "favorite" to your class and warn the librarian that it may be necessary to purchase extra copies!

ELECT A BOOK!

Boys and Girls! We are going to hold a Book Election to determine a School or Class Favorite! To help us prepare, we need to understand some of the terms we will be hearing. Use the reference section of the library to find the meanings of the following terms.

parties:_____

caucus:_____

campaign: _____

platform: _____

candidate: _____

nomination: _____

primary:_____

ballot: _____

poll:_____

precinct: _____

ballot box:_____

poll watchers: _____

voting:_____

Name(s) _____

PLATFORM WORKSHEET

Title_____ Author _____

This book is about _____
_____
_____

What do you think is the targeted age level of this book?_____
Why?_____
_____

Would both boys and girls like this book? _____
_____

The format of a book refers to its appearance: the cover, the illustrations, the print size and type, etc. Do you think the format of this book will appeal to most children? Why or why not? _____
_____

Describe the main characters (if this is a work of fiction). Are they characters that most children would like?_____
_____
_____

If this is a nonfiction book: Is the information in it easily understood? Are there parts of the book that make understanding easier (index, glossary, photographs, charts, etc.)?
_____
_____
_____

Things *some* readers might not like about this book are:_____
_____
_____

The BEST things about this book are (write a description next to each):
___ Content   _____
___ Subject   _____
___ Illustrations _____
___ Information   _____
___ Other   _____

If I were going to give a "sales pitch" for this book, I'd want to be sure to say _____
_____
_____
_____

Name(s)_____

A bulletin board display to motivate students!

A seasonal bulletin board for you! Use the information provided to plan thematic units and classroom correlations. Use the display to spark reading interest in your students!

DECEMBER BIOGRAPHIES Include:

12-3-1859 George P. Seurat
12-5-1782 Martin Van Buren
12-5-1901 Walt Disney
12-8-1765 Eli Whitney
12-9-1848 Joel Chandler Harris
12-22-1696 James Oglethorpe
12-25-1821 Clara Barton
12-25-1642 Isaac Newton
12-27-1822 Louis Pasteur
12-29-1856 Woodrow Wilson
12-29-1808 Andrew Johnson

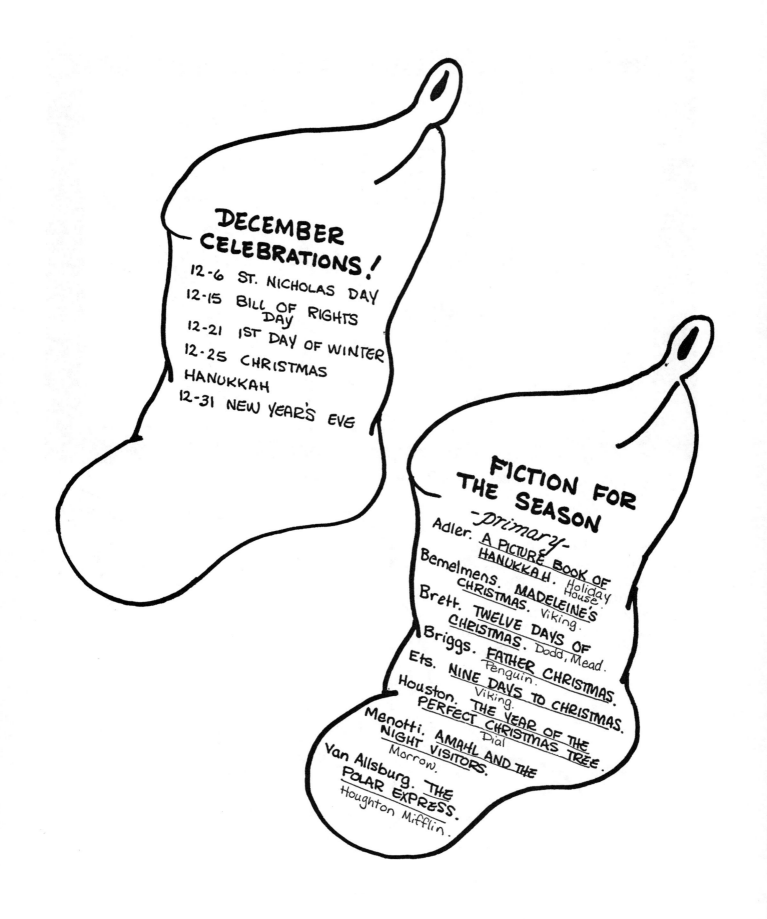

DECEMBER CELEBRATIONS!

12-6 ST. NICHOLAS DAY
12-15 BILL OF RIGHTS DAY
12-21 1ST DAY OF WINTER
12-25 CHRISTMAS
HANUKKAH
12-31 NEW YEAR'S EVE

FICTION FOR THE SEASON
-Primary-

Adler. A PICTURE BOOK OF HANUKKAH. Holiday House.
Bemelmens. MADELEINE'S CHRISTMAS. Viking.
Brett. TWELVE DAYS OF CHRISTMAS. Dodd, Mead.
Briggs. FATHER CHRISTMAS. Penguin.
Ets. NINE DAYS TO CHRISTMAS. Viking.
Houston. THE YEAR OF THE PERFECT CHRISTMAS TREE. Dial.
Menotti. AMAHL AND THE NIGHT VISITORS. Morrow.
Van Allsburg. THE POLAR EXPRESS. Houghton Mifflin.

HISTORICAL EVENTS TO READ ABOUT

12-3-1818 Illinois admitted to Union.

12-3-1967 First human heart transplant.

12-7-1941 Bombing of Pearl Harbor

12-10-1817 Mississippi admitted to Union.

12-12-1787 Pennsylvania,

12-11-1816 Indiana,

12-14-1819 Alabama' admitted to Union

12-14-1911 Amundsen reached South Pole.

12-16-1773 Boston Tea Party

12-17-1903 Wright Brothers' flight at Kitty Hawk, N.C.

12-18- New Jersey entered Union.

12-19-1777 Continental Army camped at Valley Forge.

12-21-1620 Pilgrims landed at Plymouth, Mass.

12-28-1846 Iowa entered Union

12-29-1845 Texas admitted to Union.

FICTION FOR THE SEASON
-Intermediate-

Andersen. THE FIR TREE. Harper and Row.

Burch. CHRISTMAS WITH IDA EARLY. Viking.

Caudill. A CERTAIN SMALL SHEPHERD. Rinehart, Holt, Winston.

Dickens. A CHRISTMAS CAROL IN PROSE. Holiday House.

Robinson. THE BEST CHRISTMAS PAGEANT EVER. Harper and Row.

Van Leeuwen. THE GREAT CHRISTMAS KIDNAPPING CAPER. Dial

December Book-a-tivity

a readers' reference tree!

Use your classroom Christmas tree for a little more than just decoration this year! Send students scurrying to the library to bone up on reference skills and learn more about the season with the Readers' Reference Tree!

Here's How:

1 Make copies of the ornaments on page 47, using brightly-colored paper. Fold paper in half on the dotted line and cut out the image.

2 Using the list of suggested questions on page 49, write a different question inside each ornament. (You may wish to come up with your own questions!) Number the outside of each ornament.

3 Arrange the "ornaments" among your regular ornaments on the tree.

4 Make a copy of the answer sheet (page 50) for each student. Ask the students to look for the seasonal questions on the ornaments hanging on the tree. They may use their spare time this month to do research to find the answers. It is not necessary to answer the questions in numerical order, but the number on an ornament should correspond with a number on the answer sheet.

5 Give awards to those who find all the answers just before Winter/ Christmas Break. You might offer a special treat for the FIRST student to find all the answers.

1. Copy on photocopier.

2. Fold on dotted line.

3. Cut image, making a double-sided "ornament."

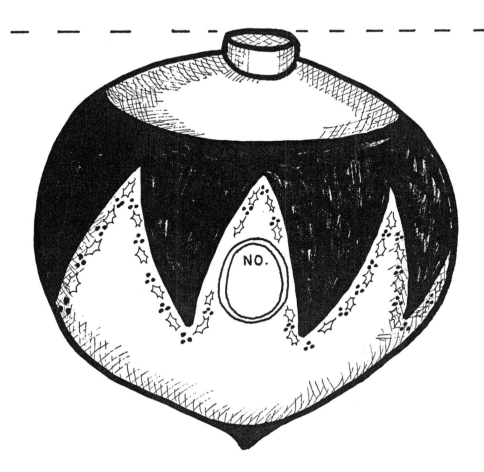

READERS' REFERENCE TREE!

READERS! The questions are on the tree, but the answers are in books! You do not have to answer the questions in order, but be *sure* the number of your answer corresponds with the number on the ornament! I HOPE YOU DO A TREE-MENDOUS JOB!

1. _____
2. _____
3. _____
4. _____
5. _____
6. _____
7. _____
8. _____
9. _____
10. _____
11. _____
12. _____
13. _____
14. _____
15. _____
16. _____
17. _____
18. _____
19. _____
20. _____

Name(s) _____

SUGGESTED QUESTIONS FOR THE READERS' REFERENCE TREE

1. How do you say "Merry Christmas" in Mexico?

2. Who is corpulent: Tiny Tim or Santa Claus?

3. Where is Christmas Island?

4. Who wrote "Silent Night"?

5. Who created the first Christmas card?

6. Who wrote *The Night Before Christmas?*

7. What newspaper editor answered Virginia's question with "Yes, Virginia, there *is* a Santa Claus"?

8. Who was Saint Nicholas?

9. How did Americans come to use the name "Santa Claus"?

10. When does the Christmas season begin in Sweden?

11. According to Clement C. Moore, what are the names of Santa's reindeer?

12. Where is the Christmas story to be found in the Bible?

13. How is the Advent wreath used in Germany?

14. Why do young people visit fountains on Christmas Eve in Switzerland?

15. How many words can you make from the letters in the word "Christmas"?

16. Name a famous painting of the Nativity and its artist.

17. What is a "menorah"?

18. What is Hanukkah?

19. When is the first day of winter?

20. What is a winterberry?

ANSWERS TO SUGGESTED QUESTIONS FOR
THE READERS' REFERENCE TREE:

1. "Feliz Navidad"
2. Santa Claus!
3. In the Indian Ocean south of Java
4. Joseph Mohr
5. John Calcott Horsley
6. Clement C. Moore
7. Frank Church of the *New York Sun*
8. A bishop of Myra (in Asia) in the A.D. 300's, known for his generosity
9. Early Dutch settlers in New York called Saint Nicholas "Sinterklaas"
10. On St. Lucia Day, December 13
11. Dasher, Dancer, Prancer, Vixen, Comet, Cupid, Donder, and Blitzen
12. Most of the story is located in Luke 2 and Matthew 1-2
13. Four candles are on the Advent wreath and one is lit on each of the four Sundays before Christmas.
14. Tradition says that if a young person takes three sips of water from each fountain on the way to midnight service, the young person's future husband or wife will be waiting at the door of the church.
15. Answers will vary.
16. There are many. Among the most well known are those by Leonardo da Vinci, Peter Paul Rubens, Albrecht Durer, Fra Angelico, Filippino Lippi, Rogier Van der Weyden, Hugo Van der Goes.
17. A candelabrum with eight branches. A candle is lit each of eight nights during Hanukkah.
18. It is a Jewish festival celebrated beginning on the eve of the 25th day of the Hebrew month of Kislev (around December). It lasts eight days.
19. December 21 or 22
20. It is a shrub that produces red berries in November. It grows in the Eastern U.S. and is similar to holly.

Congratulations, _____!

You sure SPRUCED UP your reference skills with READERS' REFERENCE TREE!

Date _____
Teacher _____

DECEMBER
The Time for "Light Reading"

With holidays and semester break approaching, it will probably be quite difficult to motivate your students to engage in some "heavy reading." BRIGHTEN UP and flow with the spirit of the season by encouraging your students to use December for "light reading"! Humorous fiction, joke and riddle books, popular children's magazines, and even comic books can count!

Children will welcome the chance to read and share "fun" reading choices. You can have a bright attractive seasonal display if you use the pattern and idea on the following page!

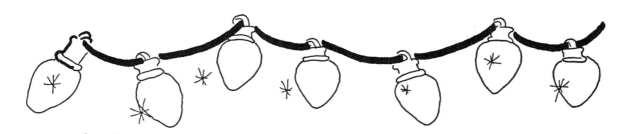

IDEA! STOCK YOUR CLASSROOM READING CORNER THIS MONTH WITH "LIGHT READING": COMICS FROM THE SUNDAY NEWSPAPER, HIGH INTEREST SUBJECT BOOKS (MOTORCYCLES, BASKETBALL, BIOGRAPHIES OF ENTERTAINMENT CELEBRITIES, ETC.), COMIC BOOKS, MAGAZINES, ETC. IT WILL BE A SEASONAL "TREAT" THAT WILL KEEP STUDENTS INTERESTED IN READING AT A TIME WHEN ATTENTION IS LIABLE TO WANDER!

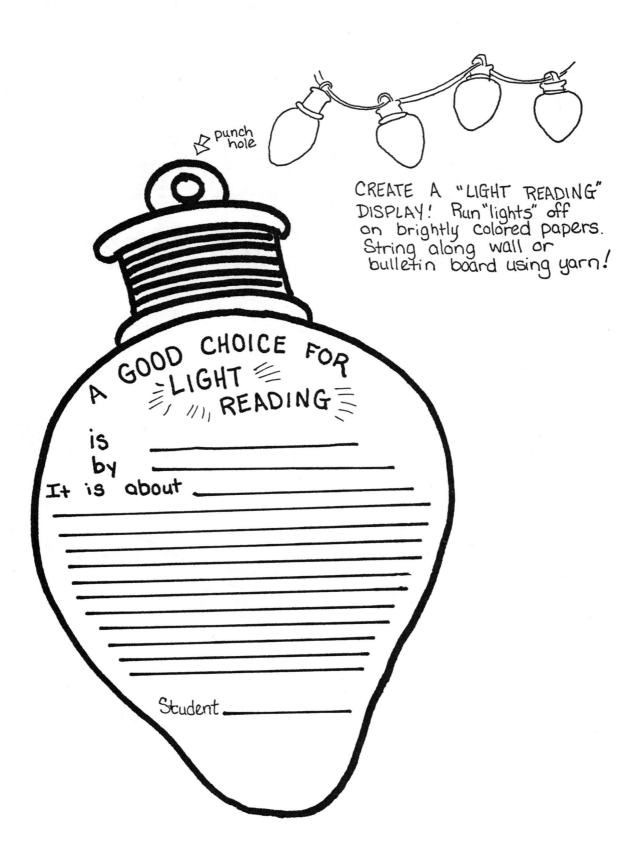

punch hole

CREATE A "LIGHT READING" DISPLAY! Run "lights" off on brightly colored papers. String along wall or bulletin board using yarn!

A GOOD CHOICE FOR LIGHT READING

is _____

by _____

It is about _____

_____
_____
_____
_____
_____
_____
_____
_____
_____
_____

Student _____

These Make MIGHTY N' ICE READING in January!

FICTION FOR THE SEASON

JAN. BIOGRAPHIES TO READ

HISTORICAL EVENTS TO READ ABOUT!

JAN. CELEBRATIONS

A bulletin board display to motivate readers!

Use the information provided to plan thematic units and classroom correlations!

JANUARY BIOGRAPHIES INCLUDE:

1-1-1735 Paul Revere
1-1-1752 Betsy Ross
1-3-1793 Lucretia Mott
1-4-1785 Jakob Grimm
1-9-1913 Richard Nixon
1-12-1737 John Hancock
1-17-1706 Benjamin Franklin
1-19-1807 Robert E. Lee

1-21-1824 "Stonewall" Jackson
1-27-1832 Lewis Carroll
1-30-1882 Franklin D. Roosevelt
1-15-1929 Martin Luther King

FICTION FOR THE SEASON:

-Primary-

Briggs. THE SNOWMAN. Random House.

DE REGNIERS. SNOW PARTY.

Hader. THE BIG SNOW. Aladdin

Keats. THE SNOWY DAY. Viking

Mendez. THE BLACK SNOWMAN. SBS.

Stock. SOMETHING IS GOING TO HAPPEN.

Stevenson. UN-HAPPY NEW YEAR, EMMA!

Tresselt. WHITE SNOW, BRIGHT SNOW. Morrow.

HISTORICAL EVENTS -TO READ ABOUT-

1-1-1863 Emancipation Proclamation

1-3-1959 Alaska 49th State

1-5-1925 1st woman governor-Nellie Ross - Wyoming

1-4-1896 Utah - 45th State

1-6-1912 New Mexico- 47th State

1-10-1920 League of Nations established

1-15-1967 First Superbowl Game

1-24-1848 Gold discovered in California

1-26-1837 Michigan- 26th state

1-27-1880 Thomas Edison issued patent for incandescent light.

1-29-1861 Kansas- 34th state

JANUARY CELEBRATIONS

1-1 NEW YEAR'S DAY
1-5 GEORGE WASHINGTON CARVER DAY
1-20 INAUGURATION DAY (every 4 years)
1-20 MARTIN LUTHER KING DAY

POETRY

Frost. STOPPING BY THE WOODS ON A SNOWY EVENING.

Prelutsky. IT'S SNOWING! IT'S SNOWING!

Bulletin board idea

Classroom "hang-up"

WEATHER TO CURL UP WITH A BOOK?

January weather can make for long, boring afternoons and weekends for your students—so invite them to beat the "blahs" by "Curling Up With A Book!" The accompanying patterns will make attractive "hang-ups" for your classroom, as well as provide an alternative form of book reporting for your students. You may also choose to use the above bulletin board idea!

Bulletin board hints:
- Use straight pins to attach cotton balls for "snowflakes."
- You may choose to hang actual "café-style" curtains.
- Using "white-it-out" or "liquid paper," paint the tops of your cut-out letters to resemble "snowcapped" letters!

Have students write their "mini-reports" in
a circular fashion, then
cut along dark
line beginning here. Attach to cat
hang-up.

Off on the Right Foot for the NEW YEAR!

Resolve to check out the LIBRARY!

It's the month for NEW YEAR'S RESOLUTIONS! Encourage your young readers to get off on the right foot by stepping into the library! This activity will insure that students examine each type of print media offered: fiction, nonfiction, biography, reference, and periodicals. It is to be hoped that students will be motivated to branch out into different reading genres, *and* will become more aware of research possibilities.

PLANNING SUGGESTIONS:

1 Invite your students to make this New Year's Resolution: "Check out the Library." Explain the terms of the Contract on pages 60-61 and give each a copy. Display the "New Year's Resolution" Scroll, page 62. (You may choose to enlarge this using an opaque projector.) Have students sign this scroll and use it to chart their progress in order to keep them goal-oriented.

2 Schedule research times for the entire class in the media center, or arrange for students to visit the media center in small groups.

3 As students complete the terms of their Contract, they will bring their assignments and Contracts to you (or to the librarian) for checking. They should also be sure to chart their progress on the "scroll."

4 Provide a small treat for those students who successfully complete the program.

You can make awards more "special" by rolling like a scroll and tying with a thin satin ribbon!

Resolve to Check Out the Library
STUDENT CONTRACT

I, _____, resolve to get off on the Right foot in ____. by resolving to "check out the library"!
I will complete the following:

☑ 1. DISCOVER FICTION. Describe the kind of order in which fiction books are kept. _____
_____

Find an author of each of the following types of fiction:
- Fantasy _____
- Mystery _____
- Realistic _____
- Historical _____
- Sports _____

☐ 2. DISCOVER NONFICTION. Describe the kind of order in which nonfiction books are arranged. _____
_____

Below, write the Dewey class name for each Dewey number and a title in that category that you discover on the shelves:

Number	Class	Title
000	_____	_____
100	_____	_____
200	_____	_____
300	_____	_____
400	_____	_____
500	_____	_____
600	_____	_____
700	_____	_____
800	_____	_____
900	_____	_____

☐ 3. What is the purpose of a reference book? _____
_____

In what kind of order are reference books arranged?_____
_____

Locate each of the following types of reference books and describe the type
of information found in each.
Atlas_____
Almanac_____
Biographical dictionary _____
Geographical dictionary_____
Thesaurus _____

☐ 4. What is the vertical file? _____
_____

In what kind of order is the vertical file arranged? _____
_____Explore the vertical file. Choose a subject. Make a list
of books or topics that are contained in the file under this subject heading.
_____

☐ 5. Name several of the magazines located in your library._____
_____

Choose two magazines for examination. How are they alike? How are they
different?_____
_____
_____

☐ 6. Discover the biography section. In what order are biographies arranged?
_____

List the names of five people who have had biographies written about
them and the reason each was famous. (Choose these people from five
different fields or professions.)

_____
_____
_____
_____
_____

Successful completion of the contract on _____

    Teacher _____

    Student _____

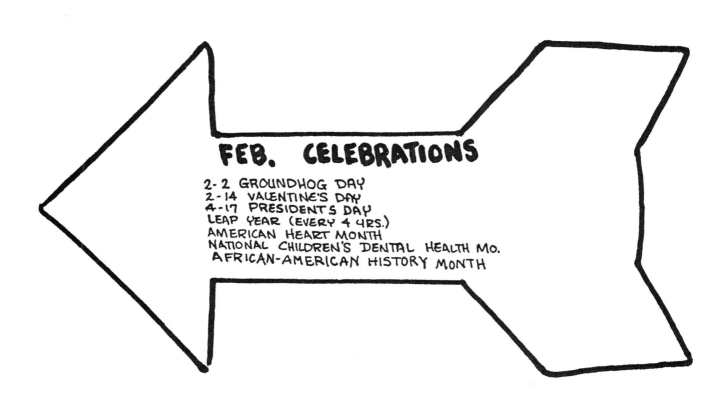

FEB. CELEBRATIONS

2-2 GROUNDHOG DAY
2-14 VALENTINE'S DAY
4-17 PRESIDENTS DAY
LEAP YEAR (EVERY 4 YRS.)
AMERICAN HEART MONTH
NATIONAL CHILDREN'S DENTAL HEALTH MO.
AFRICAN-AMERICAN HISTORY MONTH

FEBRUARY BIOGRAPHIES

2-3-1809 FELIX MENDELSSOHN
2-4-1902 CHARLES A. LINDBERGH
2-6-1756 AARON BURR
2-6-1895 "BABE RUTH"
2-9-1773 WILLIAM HENRY HARRISON
2-11-1847 THOMAS A. EDISON
2-12-1809 ABRAHAM LINCOLN
2-15-1820 SUSAN ANTHONY

2-22-1732 GEORGE WASHINGTON
2-22-1857 ROBERT BADEN-POWELL
2-25-1841 RENOIR
2-26-1846 "BUFFALO BILL" CODY

HISTORICAL EVENTS TO READ ABOUT:

2-1-1790 U.S. SUPREME COURT MET FOR 1ST TIME.
2-4-1861 CONFEDERATE STATES OF AMERICA FORMED.
2-6-1788 MASSACHUSETTS RATIFIED CONSTITUTION.
2-8-1910 BOY SCOUTS OF AMERICA INCORPORATED
2-14-1859 OREGON, 33RD STATE.
2-14-1912 ARIZONA, 48TH STATE.

2-20-1962 ASTRONAUT JOHN GLENN ORBITED EARTH 3 TIMES.
2-20-1792 U.S. POST OFFICE CREATED.

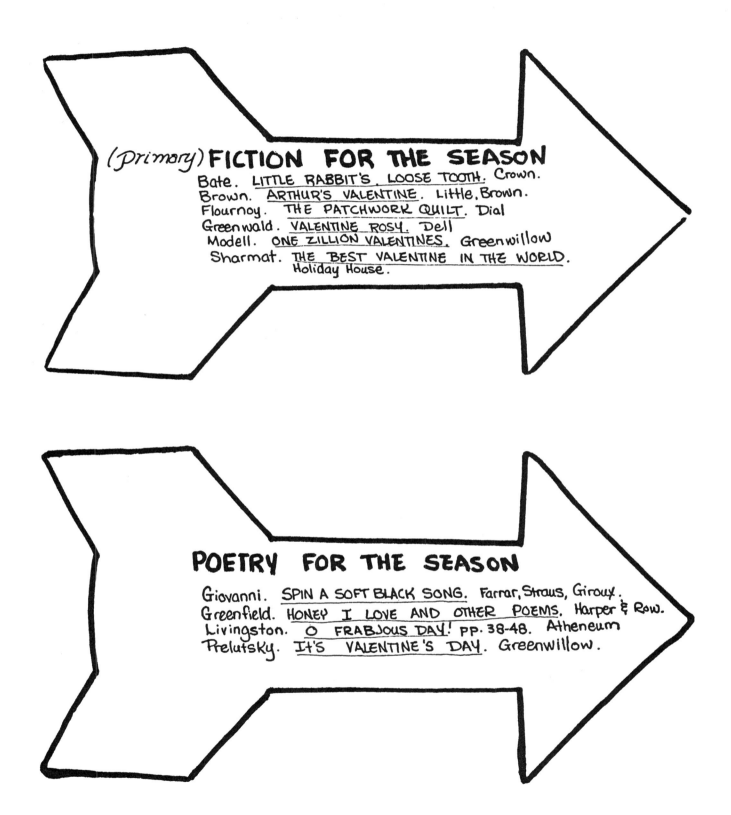

(Primary) FICTION FOR THE SEASON

Bate. LITTLE RABBIT'S LOOSE TOOTH. Crown.
Brown. ARTHUR'S VALENTINE. Little, Brown.
Flournoy. THE PATCHWORK QUILT. Dial
Greenwald. VALENTINE ROSY. Dell
Modell. ONE ZILLION VALENTINES. Greenwillow
Sharmat. THE BEST VALENTINE IN THE WORLD. Holiday House.

POETRY FOR THE SEASON

Giovanni. SPIN A SOFT BLACK SONG. Farrar, Straus, Giroux.
Greenfield. HONEY I LOVE AND OTHER POEMS. Harper & Row.
Livingston. O FRABJOUS DAY! PP. 38-48. Atheneum
Prelutsky. It's VALENTINE'S DAY. Greenwillow.

February Book-a-tivity

BOOKS WITHOUT PARTNERS!

Invite your students to have a heart—for books without partners! Children often overlook very good books because the books look old or don't have attractive covers. Launch your students on a campaign that will help them and other students in your school discover reading they might otherwise have missed! This program will make your students aware that "you can't judge a book by its cover," as well as promote book-sharing and alternative book reporting!

Here's How:

1 Ask your librarian for books on your students' reading level that are not often checked out from the library. Keep these books in the classroom for your February program or leave them in the library with small "lonely heart" stickers on their spines. Have each student choose one.

2 If students feel their books are truly good books that should not have been neglected, they are ready to take part in the "Books Without Partners" campaign!

IDEAS FOR YOUR "BOOKS WITHOUT PARTNERS" CAMPAIGN!

- Have students fill out the "This is HEARTLY a Book to Miss!" slip (page 67) and attach to the book as shown. The book should be returned to the library in order to attract other readers.

- Have the students make bright new covers for the books. Laminate these or ask the librarian for the special plastic book jackets she will be sure to have. (You might invite the librarian to the classroom to demonstrate the covering of book jackets!)

- Have your students create a video production about the "forgotten" books in your school library. Entitle it "REAL READERS DON'T MISS A BEAT." An announcement for your video is on page 68. Students may simply do oral book talks or produce a video like a TV talk show complete with character interviews and commercials that "sell the books"!

- Help students keep up with the results of their "Books Without Partners" campaign by using the "MATCHING UP READERS" idea on page 69. They will be thrilled to know that their efforts at book sharing really do pay off!

- Be sure to give each participant an award and send home a tele-parent-gram (page 70)!

THIS IS **HEARTLY** A BOOK TO MISS!

cut along dotted line

DON'T MISS THIS BOOK! THE BEST PART IS _____

_____
_____
_____
_____
_____

RECOMMENDED BY:

SLIP HEART OVER COVER OF BOOK (WHERE DOTTED LINES WERE CLIPPED) TO FLAG READERS' ATTENTION!

REAL READERS DON'T MISS A "BEAT!

_____'s class doesn't MISS A BEAT IN READING! We've discovered some VERY GOOD BOOKS in the library that have been "forgotten"!

WE'D SURE LIKE TO MATCH READERS UP WITH THEM!

Tune in to our closed circuit video:

date _____
time _____
channel _____

Hear about books HEARTLY WORTH MISSING — THEN HURRY BEFORE SOMEONE BEATS you to THEM!

HELP STUDENTS KEEP UP WITH THEIR READER - BOOK MATCH-UPS WITH THIS IDEA!

Enlist the support of your librarian (who'll be thrilled to be included in this book promotion!). Have each student write the title of the "forgotten" book he/she is promoting on one half of the broken heart below. Create a bulletin board or display of these "heart halves" entitled **MATCHING UP READERS!** On the other half, have students write the title on the back and deposit it in the book's card pocket. As the librarian checks out a book as a result of your **BOOKS WITHOUT PARTNERS CAMPAIGN,** she can have the reader sign the front of the heart half and then return the halves to you to be matched up with the "lonely half" in your display!

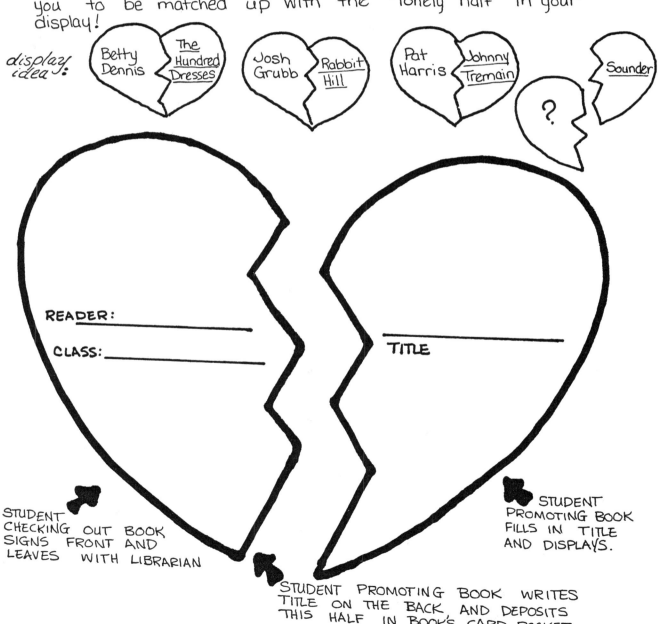

display idea:

Betty Dennis / The Hundred Dresses

Josh Grubb / Rabbit Hill

Pat Harris / Johnny Tremain

? / Sounder

READER: _____

CLASS: _____

TITLE _____

STUDENT CHECKING OUT BOOK SIGNS FRONT AND LEAVES WITH LIBRARIAN

STUDENT PROMOTING BOOK FILLS IN TITLE AND DISPLAYS.

STUDENT PROMOTING BOOK WRITES TITLE ON THE BACK AND DEPOSITS THIS HALF IN BOOK'S CARD POCKET.

YOU DIDN'T MISS A "**BEAT!**"

in our BOOKS WITHOUT PARTNERS Program!

Thanks,

_____

for outstanding participation!

date _____ teacher _____

Tele-Parent-Gram

Dear Parents,

This month your child, _____, adopted a "forgotten" book in our school library and promoted it for other readers in our **BOOKS WITHOUT PARTNERS** Program! This was HEARTLY news to keep to myself!

Date _____ Teacher _____

BOOKS TO GET
Wind of in March!

FICTION FOR THE SEASON

MARCH BIOGRAPHIES

HISTORICAL EVENTS TO READ ABOUT

MARCH CELEBRATIONS

A bulletin board bibliography to spark reading interest in your students!

Use the information provided to plan thematic units and classroom correlations.

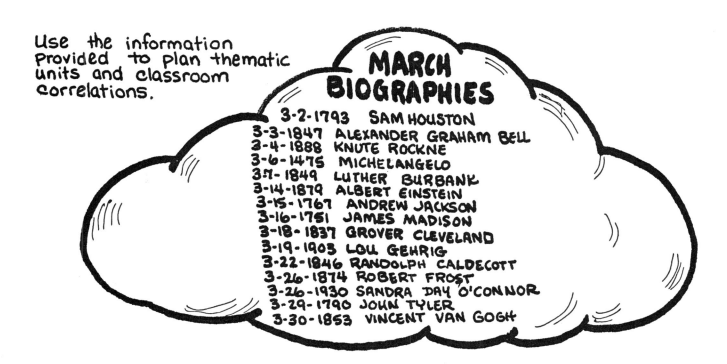

MARCH BIOGRAPHIES

3-2-1793 SAM HOUSTON
3-3-1847 ALEXANDER GRAHAM BELL
3-4-1888 KNUTE ROCKNE
3-6-1475 MICHELANGELO
3-7-1849 LUTHER BURBANK
3-14-1879 ALBERT EINSTEIN
3-15-1767 ANDREW JACKSON
3-16-1751 JAMES MADISON
3-18-1837 GROVER CLEVELAND
3-19-1903 LOU GEHRIG
3-22-1846 RANDOLPH CALDECOTT
3-26-1874 ROBERT FROST
3-26-1930 SANDRA DAY O'CONNOR
3-29-1790 JOHN TYLER
3-30-1853 VINCENT VAN GOGH

FICTION FOR THE SEASON

Balian. LEPRECHAUNS NEVER LIE. Abington.

Hutchins. THE WIND BLEW. Viking.

Craig. WINDY DAY. Troll.

McDermott. DANIEL O'ROURKE.

POETRY FOR THE SEASON

Bonner. EARLY BIRDS, EARLY WORDS. Scroll.

Brown. NIBBLE NIBBLE. Young Scott.

Fisher. LISTEN, RABBIT. Crowell.

Hopkins. ELVES, FAIRIES, & GNOMES. Knopf.

Sandburg. WIND SONG. Harcourt, Brace, & World.

MARCH CELEBRATIONS

NATIONAL WILDLIFE WEEK
FIRST DAY OF SPRING
GIRL SCOUT WEEK
RED CROSS MONTH
3-17 ST. PATRICK'S DAY
YOUTH ART MONTH

HISTORICAL EVENTS TO READ ABOUT:

3-1-1803 OHIO, 17TH STATE
3-1-1867 NEBRASKA, 37TH STATE
3-3-1845 FLORIDA, 27TH STATE
3-4-1791 VERMONT, 14TH STATE
3-6-1836 ALAMO CAPTURED
3-7-1876 TELEPHONE PATENTED BY ALEXANDER GRAHAM BELL
3-12-1912 GIRL SCOUTS FOUNDED
3-15-1820 MAINE, 23rd STATE
3-18-1959 HAWAII ADMITTED TO THE UNION
3-23-1775 PATRICK HENRY'S FAMOUS WORDS, "GIVE ME LIBERTY OR GIVE ME DEATH!"

WEAR **GREEN** IF YOU'RE A READER!

Every child is sure to wear green on St. Patrick's Day! Children can help you "push the books" by wearing the badge below. You may simply provide a badge for each child in your classroom, or you may have each child "earn" a shamrock by reading and reporting on a book—perhaps a book with a green cover, one with the word "green" in the title, or one by an author named Green!

MAKE COPIES ON BRIGHT GREEN PAPER.

THE *Leprechauns* MAY BE WATCHING!

Catch 'em reading with this idea! "The Leprechauns May Be Watching" is a St. Patrick's Day book promotion that will encourage the love of silent reading. **Here's how.**

1 Enlist the aid of several "leprechauns": cafeteria workers, fellow teachers, aides, janitors, parents, even the school principal! Have your leprechauns drop in during various "free" periods—just before school, during lunch break, during recesses, at the end of the school day, etc. Make sure you enlist the aid of more than one leprechaun. Give each leprechaun a quantity of the shamrocks on page 76.

2 Announce to your students that on St. Patrick's Day "the leprechauns might be watching" to see if they really ARE readers, and a treat might be in store if they are "caught reading." Caution students, however, that leprechauns know when students are supposed to be doing lessons, and that silent reading during lessons won't help! BUT students should carry their library books with them and read whenever they have extra time to be sure the leprechauns aren't disappointed . . . because you just never know when a leprechaun will appear!

3 At the end of the day, allow students to exchange their shamrocks for "leprechaun treasure." (Gold-foil-wrapped candy or butterscotch candy makes fine "treasure.") The number of shamrocks earned determines the number of treats. You or your helper may choose to dress as a leprechaun for the reward session (costume idea on page 77).

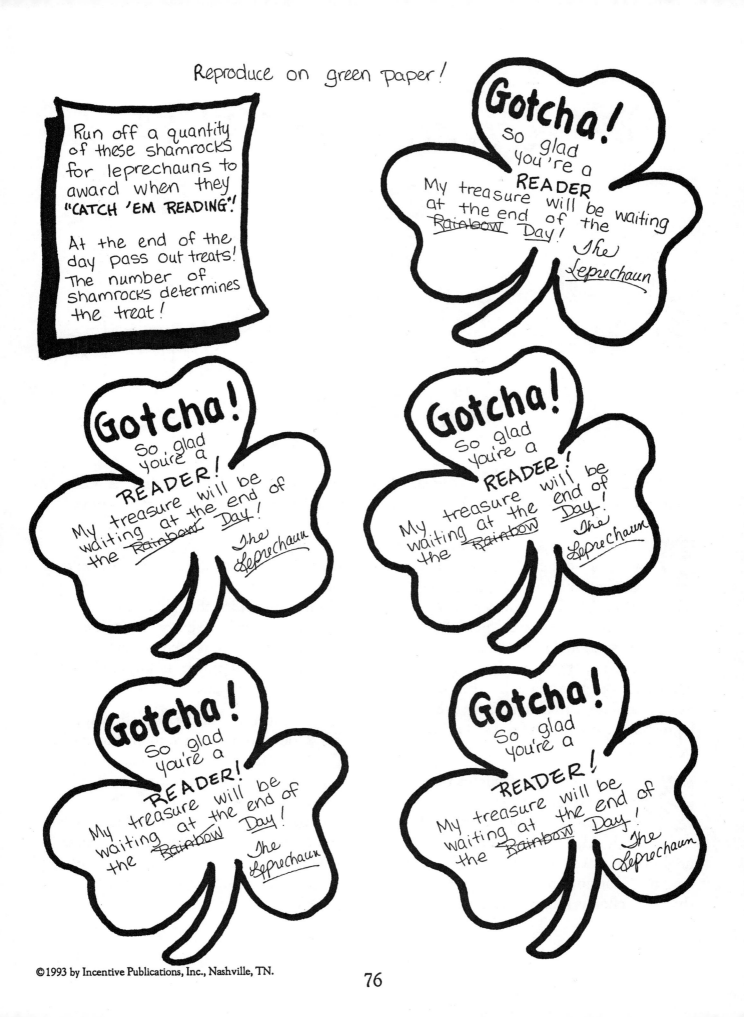

Reproduce on green paper!

Run off a quantity of these shamrocks for leprechauns to award when they "CATCH 'EM READING"!

At the end of the day pass out treats! The number of shamrocks determines the treat!

EASY-TO-MAKE (no-sew!) Leprechaun Costume!

Green plastic "derbies" are inexpensive and easy to find this time of the year.

white, black or green turtleneck

use wide belt or ribbon!

green, black or white tights or stirrup pants

② cut notches at each end.

① Cut green fett about 6' x 18" for average adult. Trim as needed.

③ Cut hole in center with slit

④ with hole puncher, punch holes each side of slit. Using thin ribbon, lace up.

⑤ Optional: using gold squeeze-bottle glitter paint create a design around neck and "hem" of tunic.

⑥ Place over head, overlap at sides, and secure using wide belt or ribbon. Sure, an' you'll be a fine leprechaun!

Cut out on dark outline - clip along dotted line leaving image in one piece.

LUCKY FIND!

BY _____

This book is a
LUCKY FIND!
You should read it
because _____
_____
_____
_____

Alternative book sharing idea:

Have students fill out the above card on favorite books, cut out and slip over the cover (as shown) to display in the media center and attract other readers!

SHOWERS of rainy day reading for April!

A bulletin board bibliography to motivate readers!

Use the information provided to plan thematic units and classroom correlations!

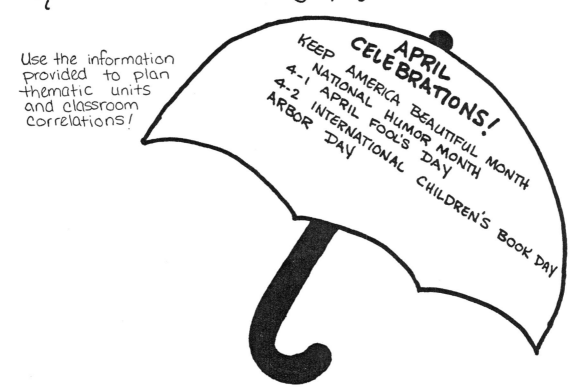

APRIL CELEBRATIONS!

KEEP AMERICA BEAUTIFUL MONTH
NATIONAL HUMOR MONTH
4-1 APRIL FOOL'S DAY
4-2 INTERNATIONAL CHILDREN'S BOOK DAY
ARBOR DAY

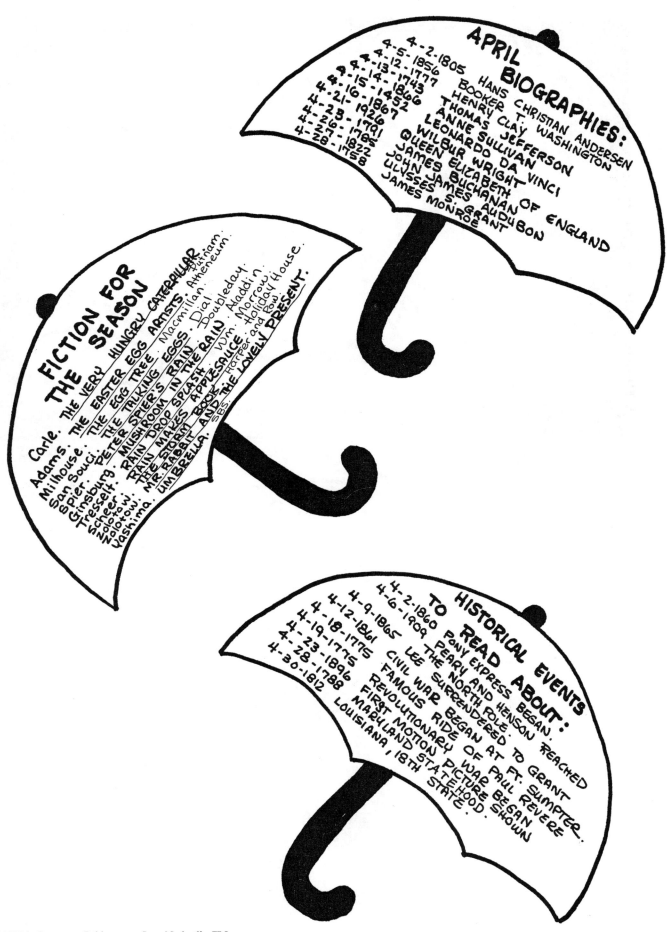

APRIL BIOGRAPHIES:
4-2-1805 Hans Christian Andersen
4-5-1856 Booker T. Washington
4-12-1777 Henry Clay
4-13-1743 Thomas Jefferson
4-14-1866 Anne Sullivan
4-15-1452 Leonardo Da Vinci
4-16-1867 Wilbur Wright
4-21-1926 Queen Elizabeth of England
4-23-1791 James Buchanan
4-26-1785 John James Audubon
4-27-1822 Ulysses S. Grant
4-28-1758 James Monroe

FICTION FOR THE SEASON
Carle. THE VERY HUNGRY CATERPILLAR. Putnam.
Adams. THE EASTER EGG ARTISTS. Macmillan/Atheneum.
Milhous. THE EGG TREE. Macmillan.
San Souci. THE TALKING EGGS. Dial.
Spier. PETER SPIER'S RAIN. Doubleday.
Ginsburg. MUSHROOM IN THE RAIN. Morrow.
Tresselt. RAIN DROP SPLASH. Aladdin.
Scheer. RAIN MAKES APPLESAUCE. Holiday House.
Zolotow. THE STORM BOOK. Harper and Row.
Yashima. UMBRELLA. Wm.
MR. RABBIT AND THE LOVELY PRESENT. SBS.

HISTORICAL EVENTS TO READ ABOUT:
4-2-1860 Pony Express Began.
4-6-1909 Peary and Henson Reached the North Pole.
4-9-1865 Lee Surrendered to Grant
4-12-1861 Civil War Began at Ft. Sumpter
4-18-1775 Famous Ride of Paul Revere
4-19-1775 Revolutionary War Began
4-23-1896 First Motion Picture Shown
4-28-1788 Maryland State Statehood
4-30-1812 Louisiana, 18th State.

April Book-a-tivity

E.A♥R.S.

E.A♥R.S: *Encouraging a Love of Reading through Student-Involvement*

Expose primary students to books and give them reading role models, and foster confidence, self-esteem, and book-sharing in intermediate children with the E.A.R.S. Program!

Here's How:

1 If you are a primary teacher, team up with an intermediate teacher. If you are an intermediate teacher, team up with a primary teacher. Pair one primary student with one intermediate student. Give each intermediate student a slip that reads:

YOUR SECRET EARS. PAL IS:

Explain to the intermediate student that the primary child will become her special reading "project," and that she will be helping to foster a love of reading in that child. Explain to each primary student that he has a special E.A.R.S. (or book) pal in a higher grade who will be sharing some very special books and reading adventures with him.

2 Have older students tell younger students about themselves, a favorite book, and favorite classroom literature activities by filling out the E.A.R.S. Sharing Forms (page 83). Each student should "mail" her form to her secret E.A.R.S. primary pal.

Have primary students fill out their E.A.R.S. Sharing Forms (page 83) and mail them to the older students.

3 Have each older student check out a favorite picture book she remembers enjoying as a child, and one she thinks her Secret E.A.R.S. pal will enjoy (based on the information on the child's Sharing Form). Have the older student practice reading the book aloud (for expression), and then make a cassette tape of the reading. Place the books and cassettes in a huge "Easter" basket with a sign reading "BASKET OF THE BEST FROM E.A.R.S. PALS."

Primary teachers, set up listening stations with headphones and cassette players in your classrooms. Throughout the day, let students take their "E.A.R.S. treat" to the listening stations and listen to the cassettes as they turn the pages of the books. Explain that the books will have to go back to the library, but the cassettes are theirs to keep.

4 As a culminating activity, have primary students write thank-you notes and invite their E.A.R.S. pals to the primary classroom for a Book-Share Party. At the party you might:
- See if primary students can guess who their E.A.R.S. pals are.
- Make snapshots of each E.A.R.S. team and give each child a copy so that he or she can remember the partnership. Or simply have them exchange school pictures.
- Have a newspaper reporter/ photographer on hand. This makes for great P.R. for your classroom.
- Show a video based on a book.
- Invite a guest storyteller to the classroom.
- Award E.A.R.S. Participation Certificates (page 84).

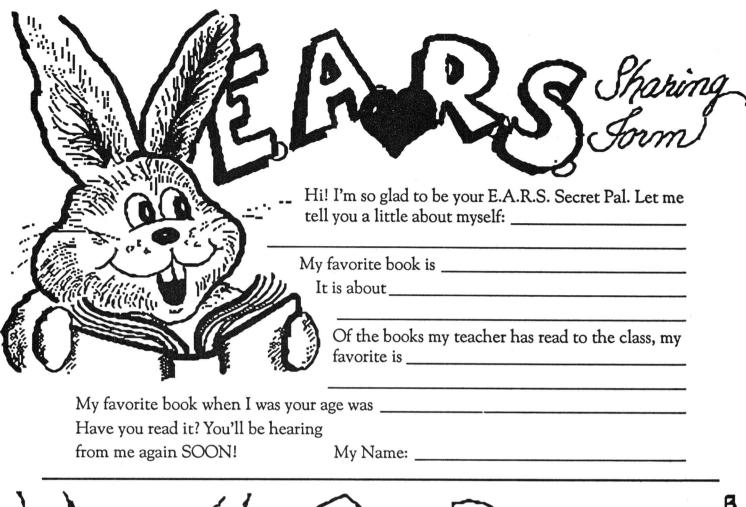

Hi! I'm so glad to be your E.A.R.S. Secret Pal. Let me tell you a little about myself: _____

_____

My favorite book is _____

It is about _____

_____

Of the books my teacher has read to the class, my favorite is _____

_____

My favorite book when I was your age was _____

Have you read it? You'll be hearing from me again SOON!

My Name: _____

Hi! I'm so glad to have you as an E.A.R.S. Secret Pal. Here is a little about myself:_____

_____

_____

I like books about_____

_____

My favorite book is _____ and I've drawn a picture about it on the back of this page. I'm looking forward to the stories you'll share with me!

My Name: _____

Thank You

for participating in the

E·A·R·S
PROGRAM!

We hope primary students enjoyed their stories and intermediate students enjoyed sharing!

_____
Teacher

_____
Date

_____
Teacher

84

Books that Kept Us IN STITCHES!

April is National Humor Month. Studies of children's book favorites consistently show that young readers are attracted to humorous fiction. So humor your students this month by asking them to read a humorous book of fiction and use a non-traditional book-reporting method.

PLANNING SUGGESTIONS:

1 Announce to students that in honor of National Humor Month they will be reading a humorous fiction book. Give each a copy of the Humorous Fiction Bibliography (page 86) to aid in book selection.

2 Go over components of a book with students and give each child a copy of "Books are Bound by Common Threads" (page 87) to help them organize their information. These may be turned in to you as "book reports."

3 Duplicate the "quilt block" pattern (page 88) for each child and have the child fill it in. These patterns might be duplicated on colored paper, or the student might use light-colored markers (yellow, light blue, etc.) to decorate the "quilt block."

4 "Piece" the blocks of your quilt together on a bulletin board. Using an opaque projector, enlarge the "threadspool" at the top of this page and put it and the slogan "Books That Kept Us in Stitches" in the center of your "quilt."

Books to Keep You IN STITCHES!

Following is a list of humorous fiction and poetry. It is by no means complete— check your media center's card catalog under the subjects HUMOROUS FICTION or HUMOROUS POETRY for more "books to keep you in stitches"!

HUMOROUS FICTION

Blume, SUPERFUDGE. Dell
Blume, TALES OF A FOURTH GRADE NOTHING. Dell.
Burch, IDA EARLY COMES OVER THE MOUNTAIN. Viking.
Cleary, HENRY HUGGINS. Avon.
Chase, THE JACK TALES. Houghton Mifflin.
Cresswell, ABSOLUTE ZERO. Viking.
Fleischman, McBROOM THE RAINMAKER. Little, Brown.
Korman, NO COINS, PLEASE! SBS.
Lindgren, PIPPI LONGSTOCKING. Viking.
McCloskey, HOMER PRICE. Viking.
Peck, PECOS BILL AND LIGHTENING. Houghton Mifflin.
Peck, SOUP. Knopf.
Pinkwater, LIZARD MUSIC. Bantam.
Robinson, THE BEST CHRISTMAS PAGEANT EVER. Harper and Row.
Rockwell, HOW TO EAT FRIED WORMS. Dell.

HUMOROUS POETRY

Hoberman, NUTS TO YOU AND NUTS TO ME: AN ALPHABET OF POEMS. Knopf.
Merriam, BLACKBERRY INK. Morrow.
Prelutsky, THE BABY UGGS ARE HATCHING. Greenwillow.
Silverstein, A LIGHT IN THE ATTIC. Harper and Row.
Silverstein, WHERE THE SIDEWALK ENDS. Harper and Row.
Tripp, MARGUERITE, GO WASH YOUR FEET. Houghton Mifflin.
Viorst, IF I WERE IN CHARGE OF THE WORLD. Aladdin.

BOOKS ARE BOUND BY COMMON *Threads!*

READERS! Use this worksheet to prepare yourself to fill in your "Quilt Block."

1. Title _____

2. Author _____

3. Illustrator (Many books will not list one—if one is listed, you'll find it on the title page.) _____

4. Publisher (on the bottom or back of the title page) _____

5. Copyright date (on the bottom or back of the title page) _____

6. Characters _____

   _____

7. Setting (where and when a story takes place) _____

   _____

8. Theme (the main idea behind a book—it could be as simple as "friendship" or "honesty") _____

   _____

9. Rising action (events in the story that help it become more exciting)

   1) _____

   2) _____

10. Climax (the most exciting part of the book) _____

11. Falling action (events in the story that take place after the climax and help the story wind to a close)

   1) _____

   2) _____

In the center of your "quilt block," draw an illustration for your story.

Name _____

Reproduce one per student.

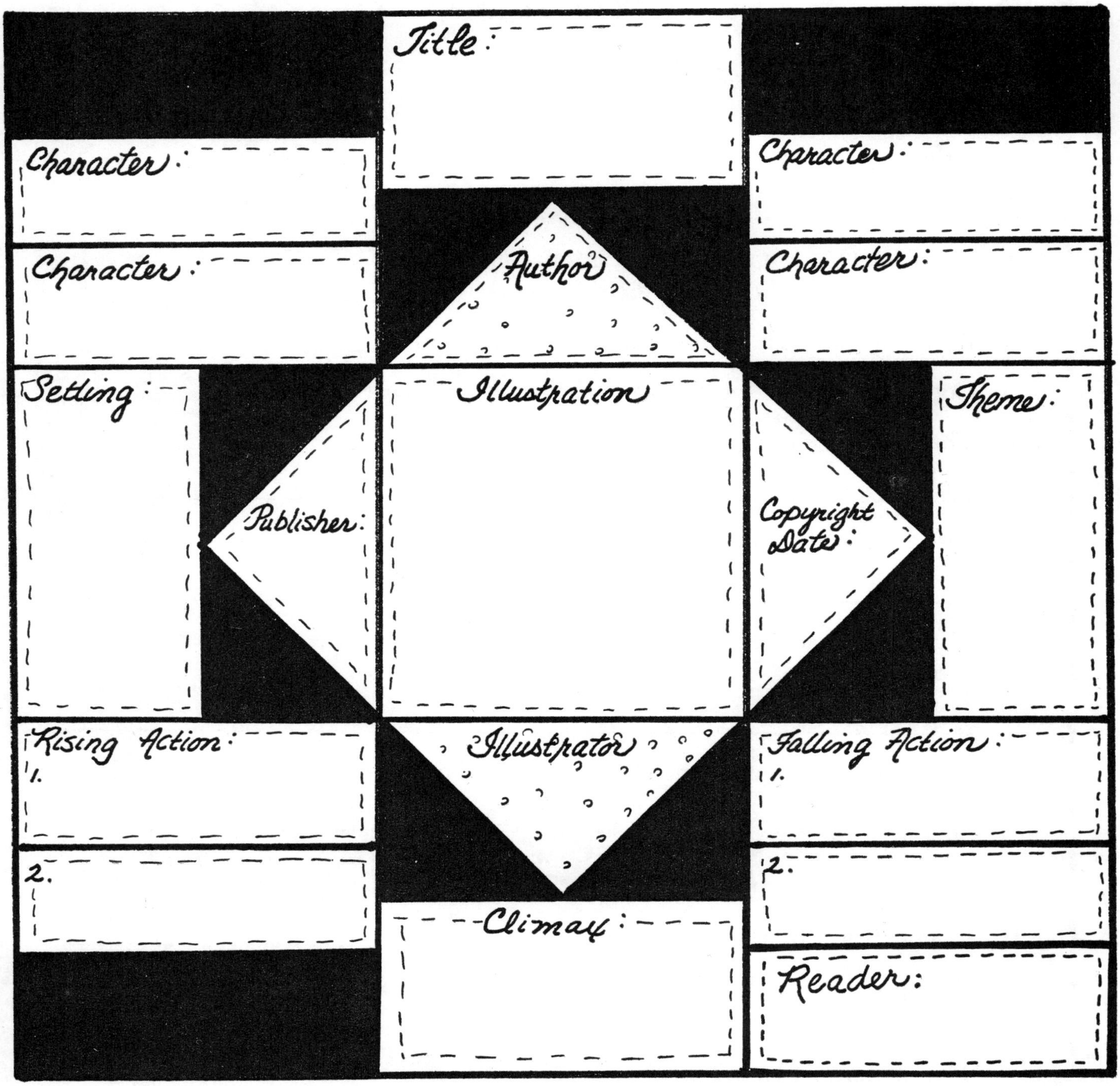

Title:

Character:

Character:

Character:

Character:

Author

Setting:

Illustration

Theme

Publisher:

Copyright
Date:

Rising Action:
1.

Illustrator

Falling Action:
1.

2.

2.

Climax:

Reader:

BASKETS of the BEST! Books for May

POETRY

BIOGRAPHIES

FICTION

A bulletin board bibliography to spark reading interest!

Use the information provided to plan thematic units and classroom correlations!

MAY CELEBRATIONS!

MAY 1 - MAY DAY
MOTHER'S DAY - 2ND SUNDAY
MEMORIAL DAY - LAST MONDAY
NATIONAL MUSIC MONTH
ARMED FORCES DAY - 3RD SAT.

POETRY FOR THE SEASON:

Prelutsky. WHAT I DID LAST SUMMER. Greenwillow
Hopkins. MOMENTS. Harcourt, Brace, Jovanovich
Behn. CRICKETS AND BULLFROGS AND WHISPERS OF THUNDER. Harcourt. B.J.
Livingston. A CIRCLE OF SEASONS. Holiday House
Prelutsky. THE BABY UGGS ARE HATCHING. Greenwillow

FICTION FOR THE SEASON — (primary)

Ehlert. PLANTING A RAINBOW. Harcourt, Brace, J.
Bunting. THE MOTHER'S DAY MICE. Houghton Mifflin
Kroll. HAPPY MOTHER'S DAY. Viking.
Aardema. WHY MOSQUITOES BUZZ IN PEOPLE'S EARS. Dial.
Udry. A TREE IS NICE. Harper and Row.
Lobel. ROSE IN MY GARDEN. SBS
Rylant. THE RELATIVES CAME. MacMillan.

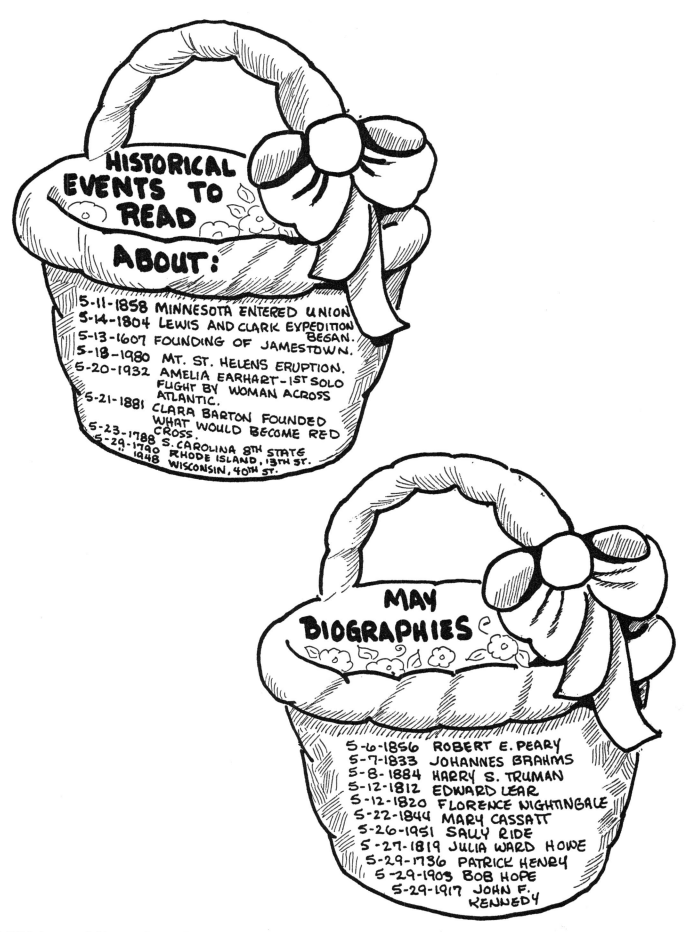

HISTORICAL EVENTS TO READ ABOUT:

5-11-1858 MINNESOTA ENTERED UNION
5-14-1804 LEWIS AND CLARK EXPEDITION BEGAN.
5-13-1607 FOUNDING OF JAMESTOWN.
5-18-1980 MT. ST. HELENS ERUPTION.
5-20-1932 AMELIA EARHART - 1ST SOLO FLIGHT BY WOMAN ACROSS ATLANTIC.
5-21-1881 CLARA BARTON FOUNDED WHAT WOULD BECOME RED CROSS.
5-23-1788 S. CAROLINA 8TH STATE
5-29-1790 RHODE ISLAND, 13TH ST.
1948 WISCONSIN, 40TH ST.

MAY BIOGRAPHIES

5-6-1856   ROBERT E. PEARY
5-7-1833   JOHANNES BRAHMS
5-8-1884   HARRY S. TRUMAN
5-12-1812 EDWARD LEAR
5-12-1820 FLORENCE NIGHTINGALE
5-22-1844 MARY CASSATT
5-26-1951 SALLY RIDE
5-27-1819 JULIA WARD HOWE
5-29-1736 PATRICK HENRY
5-29-1903 BOB HOPE
5-29-1917 JOHN F. KENNEDY

Send'em off Reading!

Tell your students to BOOK their reservations this summer! Students probably think the last thing they want to do with summer vacation is to spend it with books. But with careful planning you can plant seeds that may take root and grow as the early fun-filled days of summer stretch into long boring ones.

Here are some ideas:

- Plan a field trip to the local public library. Let students get acquainted with the library staff and facilities— you can even help them get library cards. You may allow them to go ahead and check out books!

- Request that your school library hold a book fair just before the close of school so that students can stock up on summer reading.

- Begin reading aloud a very good book chapter by chapter to your class . . . but don't finish it!

- Do a little research to find out what sorts of literature-related activities will be going on during the summer in your community: story hours, summer reading programs, storytelling, etc. Send home a parent newsletter using the newsletter heading on this page to let parents know about the activities and to let them know that you're interested in the summer reading habits of their child.

- Have each student make a list of ten things he or she plans to do during the summer—swimming, camping, vacationing, etc. Then send the student to the library to find and write down the title of a book about each of these plans. Who knows? The student may check out a book now, or a title may occur to the student later in the summer.

- For each student, duplicate a "Books to Beach For" worksheet (page 94) and the "Letter from the Teacher" and "Sun-Sational Reader Award" worksheet (page 95). Have students fill in the sandpails on the "Books to Beach For" worksheets with titles they would be interested in reading "if they get the time." Tell them if the Summer Slump hits, they can begin reading the books and check them off as they go. When a student finishes all five books, he or she can award him- or herself the "Sun-Sational Reader Award." To make this more effective, you might include with this package a self-addressed stamped envelope—and tell the students to be sure to let you know if they get the awards so that you can be proud, too!

NEWSLETTER HEADING

Parents!
BOOK AROUND THIS
SUMMER and help our
kids stay involved in books
and reading! Here are some things
I thought you might be interested
in knowing about:

Books to Beach for... and avoid the Summer Slump!!!

1.

2.

3.

4.

5.

Name(s) _____

Hey Kids!

Be a SUN-SATIONAL READER this summer! List books on the "Books to Beach for" worksheet that you would like to read. Then- when the days get long and summer slump hits ... REACH for them! Check off the titles on the right side of the pail as you read them. When you finish all five, give yourself a SUN-SATIONAL READER AWARD!

By the way, I'd like to know if you get that award!

Your Teacher,

MY AWARD for being a **Sun-SATIONAL** Reader and reading everything under the sun I intended to read this summer!

_____
date